Safe Kids
Food Safety

Dana Meachen Rau

Marshall Cavendish
Benchmark
New York

Time to make dinner!

You can help in
the kitchen.

Stop at the sink first.

Wash your hands to get rid of *germs*.

Take the food you need from the refrigerator.

Be sure to close the door!

Some foods need to stay cold.

If food is left out, it can *spoil*.

Check dates to be sure food is fresh.

Old food can make you sick.

SELL BY MAY 25

Nutrition Facts

Serving Size 2 tbsp (30g)
Servings Per Container About 15

Amount Per Serving

Calories 60   Calories from Fat 45

% **Daily Value***

Total Fat 5g   8%

Saturated Fat 3g   17%

Wash fruits and vegetables.

Everything you eat needs to be clean.

Sharp knives can hurt you.

Only cut with a grown-up's help.

Hot stoves can burn you.

Never touch the stove.

Be careful near hot pots, too.

They can bubble and splash on you.

Clean up messes
right away.

Someone could slip
on a spill.

Wash your hands again after helping.

Clean hands keep you healthy.

Clean the counters, too.

Clean the dishes and kitchen tools.

Be a safe kid with food.

Be Safe

dishes

food

hands

knife

mess

pots   **refrigerator**   **stove**

Challenge Words

germs (jurmz) Tiny living things that can make you sick.

spoil To turn rotten and unsafe to eat.

Index

Page numbers in **boldface** are illustrations.

About the Author

Dana Meachen Rau is the author of many other titles in the Bookworms series, as well as other nonfiction and early reader books. She lives in Burlington, Connecticut, with her husband and two children.

With thanks to the Reading Consultants:

Nanci Vargus, Ed.D., is an Assistant Professor of Elementary Education at the University of Indianapolis.

Beth Walker Gambro is an Adjunct Professor at the University of Saint Francis in Joliet, Illinois.

Marshall Cavendish Benchmark
99 White Plains Road
Tarrytown, New York 10591-9001
www.marshallcavendish.us

Library of Congress Cataloging-in-Publication Data

Rau, Dana Meachen, 1971-
Food safety / by Dana Meachen Rau.
p. cm. — (Bookworms: Safe kids)
Includes index.
Summary: "Identifies common food hazards and advises how to deal with them"
—Provided by publisher.
ISBN 978-0-7614-4087-1
1. Food—Juvenile literature. 2. Food—Safety measures—Juvenile literature. I. Title.
TX355.R28 2009
363.19'262—dc22
2008044934

Editor: Christina Gardeski
Publisher: Michelle Bisson
Designer: Virginia Pope
Art Director: Anahid Hamparian

Photo Research by Anne Burns Images

Cover Photo by *Corbis*/LWA Dann Tardif

The photographs in this book are used with permission and through the courtesy of:
Associated Press: pp. 1, 15, 28BL. *Photo Edit*: p. 3 Michael Newman; p. 13 David Young Wolf.
Corbis: pp. 5, 28TR Heide Benser/zefa; pp. 9, 28TC Steven Mark Needham;
pp. 17, 29R Chuck Savage; pp. 19, 29L Rainer Holz/zefa; pp. 25, 28TL Tim Pannell;
p. 27 Sean Justice. *Alamy Images*: pp. 7, 29C Paul Glendell; p. 11 David R. Frazier Photolibrary;
p. 23 Vario Images GmbH&Co.KG. *Getty Images*: pp. 21, 28BR AAGAMIA.

Printed in Malaysia
1 3 5 6 4 2

MAR - - 2010